S is for Soccer

A Fun Way to Learn Your Alphabet.

By: Harry Barker

ISBN-13: 978-1484011591

Table of Contents

This book is dedicated to my wife, Adrianna, who puts up with all my nonsense. She also manages to tolerate my four legged companions, my messy nature, and my book collection. In other words, she is the best possible companion for an ailurophile, calamitous bibliophile. And for that, I love you dearly, Sweet one.

Dedication

This book is dedicated to my wife, Adrianna, who puts up with all my nonsense. She also manages to tolerate my four legged companions, my messy nature, and my book collection. In other words, she is the best possible companion for an ailurophile, calamitous bibliophile. And for that, I love you dearly, Sweet one.
Ailurophile

A is for an ASSIST, a pass that leads to a score.

CHAPTER 2- B IS FOR BICYCLE

B is for BICYCLE kick, a play made backwards in hopes of scoring more.

CHAPTER 3- C IS FOR CORNER KICK

C is for CORNER kick,
a way to restart play.

CHAPTER 4- D IS FOR DEFENDER

D is for DEFENDER, a player who keeps the other team at bay.

Chapter 5- E is for Equalizer

E is for EQUALIZER, a goal that makes the score the same.

F is for FOUL, when someone breaks the rules of the game.

CHAPTER 7- G IS FOR GOALIE

G is for GOALIE, who saves the game it is said.

CHAPTER 8- H IS FOR HEADER

H is for HEADER, to bounce the ball off a player's head.

CHAPTER 9- I IS FOR INTERCEPT

I is for INTERCEPT, to stop the ball from finding its way.

CHAPTER 10- J IS FOR JUMPERS

J is for JUMPERS for goalpost,
to find a place to play.

CHAPTER 11- K IS FOR KICK

K is for KICK, to send the ball into the air.

CHAPTER 12- L IS FOR THE LONG BALL

L **is for LONG ball, to play the game with some flair.**

CHAPTER 13- M IS FOR MIDFIELDER

M is for MIDFIELDER, when to guard the center a player is picked.

Chapter 14- N is for NUTMEG

N is for NUTMEG, when a ball through another player's legs is kicked.

Chapter 15- O is for OFFSIDE

O is for OFFSIDE, when a player is someplace they should not be.

CHAPTER 16- P IS FOR PARALYMPIC

P is for PARALYMPIC soccer, so everyone can play and be free.

CHAPTER 17- Q IS FOR QUICK

Q **is for QUICK, to be fast and chase the ball.**

CHAPTER 18- R IS FOR REFEREES

R

is for REFEREES, to judge
the game so it is fair for all.

CHAPTER 19- S IS FOR SAVE

S is for SAVE, when the goalie prevents the ball from going in.

CHAPTER 20- T IS FOR TACKLE

T is for TACKLE, a way for a player to get the ball back again.

Chapter 21- U is for Underdogs

U is for UNDERDOGS, where the winning spirit may be found.

CHAPTER 22- V IS FOR VOLLEY

V is for VOLLEY, to kick the ball before it touches down.

CHAPTER 23- W IS FOR WALL

W
is for WALL, a defense made up of a row of players.

CHAPTER 24- X IS FOR EXRA POINT

X is for eXtra point attempt, when gotten will stop the 'nay'-sayers.

CHAPTER 25- Y IS FOR YOUTH

Y is for YOUTH, all of whom have such fun.

CHAPTER 26- Z IS FOR ZZZZ

Z is for ZZZZ, the nap after the game is done.

Harry Barker

ABOUT THE AUTHOR

Harry Barker's ABC Basketball Book is a fun way to turn learning the alphabet into an enjoyable experience. Using of the world's most popular sport as a background, Harry has created a memorable experience for young minds to connect words and vibrant pictures with the action of basketball. This results in a quick connection between ABC and fun, and leave children wanting more.

In the future, Harry will be doing many more ABC Alphabet books with the goal of entertaining young minds. His amusing way with words tied with vibrant, colored pictures is guaranteed to keep the young learners interested and are a 'must have' for any child's first ABC reader or personal book collection.

So join the fun and watch for more ABC Sport Alphabet books from Harry!

OTHER BOOKS BY HARRY BARKER

B is for BASEBALL

B is for BASKETBALL

Additional alphabet sports books coming soon!

Publishers Notes

Happy Home Publishing
863 Flat Shoals Road, STE C-360, Conyers, GA 30094, USA
HappyHomePublishing.com

CPSIA information can be obtained
at www.ICGtesting.com
Printed in the USA
LVIC06n0042300915
456294LV00006B/29